T0064562

# "PERFECT PEACE VIII"

Isaiah 26:3-4

# "PERFECT PEACE VIII"

*Prayer*

### VANESSA RAYNER

authorHOUSE®

## A Gift

*Presented to*

_____

*From*

_____

*Date*

_____

*You are valuable, not because of who you are;*
*But because of whose you are.*

AuthorHouse™
1663 Liberty Drive
Bloomington, IN 47403
www.authorhouse.com
Phone: 1 (800) 839-8640

Published by AuthorHouse   05/18/2015

ISBN: 978-1-5049-1276-1 (sc)
ISBN: 978-1-5049-1275-4 (e)

Print information available on the last page.

The Scriptures' quotations are taken from the KJV, NIV, and NLT.

The King James Version present on the Bible Gateway matches the
1987 printing. The KJV is public domain in the United States.

The Holy Bible, New International Version®, NIV® Copyright © 1973, 1978,
1984, 2011 by Biblica, Inc. Used by permission. All rights reserved worldwide.

Scripture quotations marked (NLT) are taken from the Holy Bible,
New Living Translation, copyright © 1996, 2004, 2007 by Tyndale
House Foundation. Used by permission of Tyndale House Publishers,
Inc., Carol Stream, Illinois 60188. All rights reserved.

# Contents

## Theme

The universal message of this book is the verses from Isaiah 26:3 – 4 concerning "Perfect Peace." This is the distinct and unifying composition of this book with the subtitle <u>Prayer</u>.

Thou wilt keep him in perfect peace, whose mind is stayed on thee: because he trusteth in thee. Trust ye in the LORD for ever: for in the LORD JEHOVAH is everlasting strength. Isaiah 26:3-4 KJV

You will keep in perfect peace those whose minds are steadfast, because they trust in you. Trust in the LORD forever, for the LORD, the LORD himself, is the Rock eternal. Isaiah 26:3-4 NIV

You will keep in perfect peace all who trust in you, all whose thoughts are fixed on you! Trust in the Lord always, for the Lord God is the eternal Rock. Isaiah 26:3-4 NLT

Remember, we learnt from Isaiah 26:3-4, "Perfect Peace" ~ <u>The Last Single-Digit</u> that Bible translations fall into three categories? They are Formal Equivalence, Functional Equivalence, and Paraphrase.

**Formal Equivalence** is translating words by finding reasonable words and phrases that have equal value, or meaning; while following the source language as closely as possible. This style is often referred to as "Literal Translation" or "Word-for-Word Translation." Some of the Formal Equivalence translations in English are KJV, ASV, ERV, NASB, ESV, and AMP.

**Functional Equivalence** is sometimes called "Dynamic Equivalence" or "Thought–for–Thought Translation." It is a translation process in which the translator(s) attempts to reflect and focus on the thought of the writer in the source language rather than the word-for-word translation. The NIV, HCSB, and CEV are some of the popular Functional Equivalence translations.

**The Extensive use of Dynamic Equivalence** is called a paraphrase, or thought–for–thought translation. It goes even further than dynamic equivalence when translating the source. It conveys some key concepts while not retaining even a dynamic equivalence with the text. Two popular versions of this type are NLT and MSG.

# Prayer

Father God,
I pray that this book will help your people,
open their mind, heart, and soul to You
several times throughout the day.

Father God,
bless those that help make
Your Work and Word able to go forth
in this world.

Father,
You make it clear
that You will reward those that bless your servant.
It could be by prayer, words of
encourage, buying a book,
E-mailing or twittering others about the book,
to even given that person a cup of water.

***And whosoever* shall give to drink
unto one of these little ones
a cup of cold water only in
the name of a disciple,
verily I say unto you, he shall in
no wise lose his reward.**
Matthew 10:42 KJV

**And if you give even a cup of cold water
to one of the least of my followers,
You will surely be rewarded.**

Matthew 10:42 NLT

Amen

# Author's Notes

Author notes normally provide a way to add extra information to one's book that may be awkward and inappropriate to include in the text of the book itself. It provides supplemental contextual details on the aspects of the book that are not discussed directly. It can help readers understand the content and the background details of the book better. The times and dates of researching, reading, and gathering this information are not included; only when I typed on it.

Wednesday, 24 July 2013; 1243. On the evening of July 23, 2013 around 1921, I was truly blessed, strengthened, and encouraged by Evangelist Claretha Simmons-Dessuaso on the telephone prayer line. It blessed my soul, gave me strength to face obstacles bravely, and encouraged me to finished proof-reading book title "2541." While I was on the prayer line, Father God places in my spirit a title for another book, "Prayer." Thursday, 16 October 2014; 2308. Here at last. Just finished Isaiah 26:3-4 "Perfect Peace VII," Eleven.
Saturday, 13 December 2014; 2114. The aspects of "Prayer" is so, so, very deep. It's truly overwhelming to me; help me Father God decides what to place in Your book. Your servant, vanessa. Amen.
Sunday, 4 January 2015; 0715

Tuesday, 7 January 2015; 0625; I just got home from work, must work on this book a little every day, Father God. Please, give me the desire and strength in Jesus' name. Amen.

Monday, 12 January 2015; 0305

Sunday, 25 January 2015; 0451; I'm at home with the Flu until 28th. Father God, I thank you in Jesus' name. I would be in the hospital with the Flu. Hallelujah!!!

Monday, 26 January 2015; 0543

Tuesday, 27 January 2015; 0657

Wednesday, 28 January 2015; 0704

Monday, 9 March 2015; 0707; I saw a falling Star Saturday night (March 7) as I was getting in my car for work about 2103. I made a wish to have a burning desire to type on this book every day until it's finished; even if it just one sentence.

Tuesday, 10 March 2015; 0724

Wednesday, 11 March 2015; 1431

Thursday, 12 March 2015; 0647

Friday, 13 March 2015; 0615

Saturday, 14 March 2015; 0738

Sunday, 15 March 2015; 1353

Monday, 16 March 2015; 1746

Tuesday, 17 March 2015; 0635

Wednesday, 18 March 2015; 0011; Pressing on in Jesus' Name; not feeling well.

Thursday, 19 March 2015; 1401

Friday, 20 March 2015; 1545

Saturday, 21 March 2015: 1524; Charlie Wilson' Forever Tour at the FedEx Forum was Awesome, last night. Charlie Wilson, Joe, and KEM took time to Honor Father God and speak of God's Grace & Mercy; where He brought them from and through.

Sunday, 22 March 2015; 0956

Monday, 23 March 2015; 1058

Tuesday, 24 March 2015; 1146

Wednesday, 25 March 2015; 1633; It's my B'day, It's my B'day

Thursday, 26 March 2015; 1139

Friday, 27 March 2015; 1021

Saturday, 28 March 2015; 0851

Sunday, 29 March 2015; 1012

Monday, 30 March 2015; 0847

Tuesday, 31 March 2015; 0728

Wednesday, 1 April 2015; 1919

Thursday, 2 April 2015; 1749; Today is the day. Glory Hallelujah!

Saturday, 25 April 2015; AuthorHouse wants me to make a few changes, basically three.

Monday, 11 May 2015; 0645; Got to make an adjustment on the "Thanks" page.

# Preface

Isaiah 26:3-4, "Perfect Peace VIII" ~ <u>Prayer</u>

This is the 8<sup>th</sup> book of a series of Isaiah 26:3-4, "Perfect Peace" collection. I give God all the Glory, Saints! It started from how I drew near to the Lord in my workplace by keeping my mind on Him.

**Submit yourselves therefore to God.**
**Resist the devil, and he will flee from you.**
**Draw nigh to God, and he will draw nigh to you.**
James 4:7-8 KJV

This book with the subtitle <u>Prayer</u>, focus on events that surround the word "Prayer." The word "Prayer" will forever be viewed by you in a unique way whenever you see the word. Discover the power of the Holy Spirit by relating "Prayer" to numbers, words, places, people, and things; in order to obtain "Perfect Peace" in any situation.

Remember, the LORD Jesus promised us tribulation while we were in this world.

*These things, I have spoken unto you,*
*that in me ye might have peace.*
*In the world ye shall have tribulation:*

*But be of good cheer; I have overcome the world.*
John 16:33 KJV

However, we have been promised His peace while we endure these trials, tribulations, troubles, and tests. Perfect Peace is given only to those whose mind and heart reclines upon the LORD. God's peace is increased in us according to the knowledge the LORD gives to us from His Word.

*Grace and peace be multiplied unto you*
*through the knowledge of God,*
*and of Jesus our LORD.*
2 Peter 1:2 KJV

It is our hope that you will have an in-depth understanding of various prayers, events, and informal information that surrounds the word "Prayer."

## Thanks . . . . . .      D.B.

Remember Christians, we may not know until we get to heaven just how much a song you have sung, or a book you suggested someone to read lifted their spirit man. The kind words you spoke, texted, e-mailed or tweeted bless the soul of someone you don't even know. The kind words could even be in the form of a "custom review," in which you took the time to write and post.

A customer review was written on April 21, 2014 on Amazon.com. The reviewer states, she loves to read Bible stories, the book she read was a great book, and it helped her to understand the scriptures better.

P.S.: The book she is referring to is Isaiah 26:3-4, "Perfect Peace VI" Zacchaeus. Please take time to go to Amazon.com and read the review. It's copyrighted, so AuthorHouse couldn't allow me to place it in the book.

Thanks for your support, readers; and a Special Thanks to D.B., whom I never met, conversed with or texted. May the Lord richly bless you all.

### <u>I must tell it! I just can't hold it in!</u>
I want you to understand how God knows when and how to lift your sunken spirit and increase your

dwindling faith, and bless your soul without money or material things. There are times, even as a Christians, we are completely baffled by what's happening in our lives, especially when you know you are striving to do His will.

On 03/10/15, as I was preparing to go to work about 2045 hours, I wanted to look up the other books published dates, so I went to the internet. I went to Barnes and Nobles.com, first. For some unexplained reasons, "Glory be to God" I decided to check the dates on Amazon.com, to my surprise I saw I had a review. My heart "skipped a beat," as I read my **ONLY** customer review.

The notes in Author's Notes Section dated 01/07/15 and 03/09/15 indicate how I being struggling to stay focus doing my divine calling, through the heartaches, headaches, and the lack of desire, lately. I would work on this book for 8 minutes or so, then tell myself I do more when I get a nap; but wouldn't. I know I need to believe and keep walking in God's word. I had been calling Father for help, strength, and the desire to do His will and the assignment(s) He has for me.

*** Tuesday, 7 January 2015; 0625; I just got home from work, must work on this book a little every day, Father God. Please, give me the desire and strength in Jesus' name. Amen.

***Monday, 9 March 2015; 0707; I saw a falling star Saturday night (March 7) as I was getting in my car for work about 2103. I made a wish to have a burning desire to type on this book every day until it's finished; even if it just one sentence.

Low and behold, I saw the "Customer Review" that consist of THREE short sentences, with words of encouragement, have set me a blazing!

The Unction of the Holy Spirt says, "One sentence is from the Father, One sentence is from the Son, and One sentence is from the Holy Spirit." "Shaimordshekea" (I guess the spelling because it's not in a dictionary. Those are words/utterances that flowed from my spirit to Father God' spirit when He whispers in my ear where the three sentences came from. Hallelujah is the Highest Praise!; 1 Corinthians 14:2)

Even though, the customer review was given April 21, 2014; I didn't know it exists until March 10, 2015, almost a year later. I'm reassured and motivated; my work for Father God is not in vain, just by one review. God is wonderful! He an Awesome God! Praise the Lord, Praise the LORD!

## Acknowledgement

I would like to express my gratitude to all of God's people for making this possible, by their support.

Thank and remember, "The gifts of God are in YOU" rather you chose to use them or not.

**For the gifts and calling of God
are without repentance.**
Romans 11:29 KJV

I prayer that Father God give you the strength and courage to step out on FAITH. You can do it! You can do it in Jesus' name.

**I can do all things through Christ
which strengtheneth me.**
Philippians 4:13 KJV

Thanks and May God Bless You, Greatly!

# Introduction

### *For Those Who Want to be Kept in*
### *"Perfect Peace" ~ God's Perfect Peace*

This book was prepared to open your mind to "Perfect Peace" that comes only from God and His word. It strives to raise you into a "Unique and Profound" awareness of God's presence around you at all time.

According to some people, it seems impossible to keep your mind on the LORD Jesus Christ. While most Christians will agree that if you keep your mind stayed on the LORD, he will keep you in "Perfect Peace." So many people enjoy going to church on Sundays and attending midweek services for the peace it gives, but it only last a short time.

You can experience the peace of God throughout the day and every day. His unspeakable joy, his strength, his "Perfect Peace" in the midst of the turbulent storm whether it's at work, home, college, school, etc. You can also experience this peace, even when your day is going well.

This book concept was placed in my spirit by our Father, to help me. I was being tested at my workplace while he molded me into a MAP; (Minister/Ambassador/Pastor).

Throughout these pages will be events and facts that is about and surrounds "Prayer' in a unique way. I will show you how to keep your mind on the LORD by sharing this topic in a unique manner. However, much more can be said about "Prayer" so these examples serve merely as an introduction and are not exhaustive by any means.

In the other books to follow, I will concentrate on a topic, a number, or set of numbers or a passage of scriptures. Be enlightened and enjoy the peace it will bring in Jesus' Name. Watch, what happens when you strive to keep your mind on Father God, the majority of the day.

## Dedication

I would like to dedicate Isaiah 26:3-4 "Perfect Peace VIII" <u>Prayer</u> to Evangelist Claretha Simmons-Dessauso. On the evening of July 23, 2013 around 1921 hour, I was truly blessed, strengthen and encouraged by Evangelist Claretha Simmons-Dessauso's telephone prayer line.

It blessed my soul, gave me strength to face obstacles bravely and encouraged me to finished proof-reading the book title Isaiah 26:3-4 "Perfect Peace V" 2541. While I on the prayer line, Father God places in my spirit a title for another book title "Prayer."

# Chapter 1

*The Word "Prayer"*

The words pray, prayed, praying, prayers, prayest and prayeth all appears in the King James Bible, along with "prayer." The King James Bible consists of 66 different books. They are composed by writers of various social backgrounds, in three different languages (Hebrew, Aramaic and Greek), under different circumstances over a period of about 1600 years. The 66 books of the Bible are divided into the Old Testament that contains 39 books, and the New Testament which contains 27 books.

The word pray appears 306 times in the King James Bible, and sometimes twice in a verse. It is mentioned 245 times in the Old Testament and 61 times in the New Testament. The word prayed appears 65 times in the Bible, 31 times in the Old Testament and 34 times in the New Testament. The word praying appears 20 times in the Bible, 14 times in New Testament and 6 times in the Old Testament. The word prayers appear 24 times in the Bible, 22 times in the New Testament and 2 times in the Old Testament. The word prayest appears only twice in the New Testament. The word prayeth appears 7 times in the Bible, 3 times in the New Testament and 4 times in the Old Testament.

The word "prayer" appears 104 times in the King James Bible, 31 times in New Testament and 73 times in the Old Testament. The word "prayer" is mentioned in only ten books of the 27 books of the New Testament. They are Matthew, Mark, Luke, Acts, Romans, 1 Corinthians, 2 Corinthians, Ephesians, Philippians and Colossians.

The Latin word "precari" which means "to beg, implore, and entreat" is where the English word for "prayer" originated from. Now, what is the main word in the meaning of beg, implore and entreat?

> *Beg is to ask someone earnestly*
> *or humbly for something.*
> *Implore is to beg someone earnestly*
> *or desperately to do something.*
> *Entreat is to ask someone earnestly*
> *or anxiously to do something.*
>
> Answer in back of book . . .

However, the Hebrew word for "prayer" is much more intriguing. The Hebrew word for "prayer" is "tefilah." It means "to judge." Tefilah is when a person takes the time to focus on himself. It's a time of self-evaluation and self-judgement. A person goes within himself to

2

see what he needs from God. The individual tries to understand their purpose, what's they are all about, what are their faults, and what are their qualities. This self-assessment happens through "tefilah." Tefilah also means "attachment."

People mentioned in the Bible prayed in and for many circumstances. Some prayers were for advice, for others, for their transgressions, healing, and victory over their enemies. To my surprise "prayer" is not mentioned in the Ten Commandments, (Exodus 20:1:17); nor the books of the law. At 5:20, 1/25/15 . . . I just feel the need to ask this question, "What are the ten commandments? Just pray for me . . . smile

1. _____
2. _____
3. _____
4. _____
5. Honor your father and your mother.
6. _____
7. _____
8. _____
9. You shall not bear false witness against your neighbour.
10. _____

Answers in the back

The Ten Commandments are guidelines for Christian behaviour in nearly all forms of Christianity.

3

The Gospels makes many references to Jesus praying: And when he had sent the multitudes away, he (Jesus) went up into a mountain apart to pray: and when the evening was come, he was there alone. Matthew 14:23 KJV

Then Jesus went with his disciples to a place called Gethsemane, and he said to them, "Sit here while I go over there and pray." Matthew 26:36 NIV

Before daybreak the next morning, Jesus got up and went out to an isolated place to pray. Mark 1:35 NLT

Now when all the people were baptized, it came to pass, that Jesus also being baptized, and praying, the heaven was opened. Luke 3:21 KJV

But Jesus often withdrew to lonely places and prayed. Luke 5:16 NIV

One day soon afterward Jesus went up on a mountain to pray, and he prayed to God all night. Luke 6:12 NLT

And it came to pass, as he (Jesus) was alone praying, his disciples were with him: and he asked them, saying, Whom say the people that I am? Luke 9:18 KJV
Jesus went out as usual to the Mount of Olives, and his disciples followed him. On reaching the place, he

4

said to them, "Pray that you will not fall into temptation."
Luke 22:39-40 NIV

He (Jesus) walked away, about a stone's throw, and knelt down and prayed, "Father, if you are willing, please take this cup of suffering away from me. Yet I want your will to be done, not mine." Luke 22:41-42 NLT

I had to come back to this page and add these two verses, I just had to: Then an angel from heaven appeared and strengthened him (Jesus). He prayed more fervently, and he was in such agony of spirit that his sweat fell to the ground like great drops of blood. Luke 22: 43-44 NLT

Glory

Glory

Glory

Don't just read it; Say it out loud . . . .Glory,    Glory,    Glory

## Chapter 2

*The "Lord's Prayer"*

The "Lord's Prayer" is considered the most important prayer in Christianity. Prayer is the opening of one's heart, spirit, and soul in a conversation with God. It expresses our faith in a relationship with God. It is also, us thanking and praising God for all that he has done. The "Lord's Prayer" is also called "Our Father" and the "Pater Noster" prayer. Pater Noster mean "Our Father" in Latin and it is also the first two words of the "Lord' Prayer."

Many Catholics refer to the "Our Father" as the "Pater Noster" because they pray in Latin. The Catholic Christians pray in Latin because it is the official language of the Catholic Church, but God hears our pray in any language.

**The Lord is far from the wicked,**
**but he hears the prayer of the righteous.**
Proverbs 15:29 NIV


**We know that God does not listen to sinners.**
**He listens to the godly person who does his will.**
John 9:31 NIV

Jesus taught the "Lord's Prayer" to his disciples in Aramaic.

I just can't resist . . . prayforme . . . name the first 12 disciples

1. _____
2. _____
3. _____
4. _____
5. _____
6. _____
7. _____
8. _____
9. _____
10. _____
11. _____
12. _____

Answer in back of book

The "Lord's Prayer" has been recorded in the New Testament. It's in two of the four gospels in two different manners. The "Lord's Prayer" in the Gospel of Matthew is longer than Luke's version. It was part of the "Sermon on the Mount" message taught by Jesus. The Gospel of Luke records a shorter version that is a response Jesus gave to one of his disciples who asked him to teach them to pray.

**And it came to pass, that,**
**as he was praying in a certain place,**
**when he cease, one of his**
**disciples said unto him,**
**Lord, teach us to pray, as John**
**also taught his disciples.**
Luke 11:1 KJV

The Lord's Prayers from the King James Version:

| **The Prayer in Matthew 6:9-13** | **The Prayer in Luke 11:2-4** |
|---|---|
| Our Father which art in heaven, | Our Father which art in heaven, |
| Hallowed be thy name. | Hallowed be thy name. |
| Thy kingdom come, | Thy kingdom come. |
| Thy will be done in earth, as it is in heaven. | Thy will be done, as in heaven, so in earth. |
| Give us this day our daily bread. | Give us each day our daily bread. |
| And forgive us our debts, as we forgive our debtors. | And forgive us our sins; For we also forgive every one that is indebted to us. |
| And lead us not into temptation, | And lead us not into temptation; |
| but deliver us from evil: For thine is the kingdom, and the power, and the | But deliver us from evil. |

glory, for ever. Amen.


The Lord's Prayer consists of an introduction, seventh petition and a doxology. The introduction is "Our Father, who art in heaven." The seven petitions are as follow:

| | |
|---|---|
| First | "Hallowed by thy name" |
| Second | "Thy kingdom come" |
| Third | "Thy will be done" |
| Fourth | "Give us this day our daily bread" |
| Fifth | "And forgive us our debts, as we forgive our debtors" (or "And forgive us our trespasses, as we forgive them that trespass against us") |
| Sixth | "And lead us not into temptation" |
| Seventh | "But deliver us from evil" |

The Doxology is "For thine is the kingdom, and the power, and the glory, for ever and ever. Amen."

| | |
|---|---|
| Note: | A doxology is not contained in Luke's version. |


The "Lord's Prayer" is a manner on how to pray, rather than something to be learned and recited by memorization, often without full comprehension. It is the most loved and spoken prayers in the world, written and spoken in several languages. The "Lord's Prayer" is definite a good starting points for "born again" believers.

The New Testament records Jesus, and his disciples praying on several occasions, but never this particular prayer.

Dr. V loves to express the Lord's Prayer as follows: (just pray & smile . . .)

| | |
|---|---|
| Our Father | - A personal relationship with God |
| Who art in heaven | - Faith |
| Hallowed be thy name | - Worship |
| Thy Kingdom come | - Expectation |
| Thy will be done on earth as it is in Heaven | - Submission |
| Give us this day our daily bread | – Petition |
| And forgive us our debts | – Confession |
| As we forgive our debtors | – Compassion |
| Lead us not into temptation but deliver us from evil | - Dependence |
| For thine is the kingdom, the power and the glory forever | -Acknowledgement |

# Chapter 3

*Type of Prayers*

The Bible has many types of prayers. Listed below are the titles given to describe some of the prayers, along with the verse(s) that generated that title.

1.  The Prayer of Faith:
And the prayer of faith will save the sick, and the Lord shall raise him up; and if he have committed sins, they shall be forgiven him. James 5:15 KJV

2.  Corporate Prayer:
They all joined together constantly in prayer, along with the women and Mary the mother of Jesus, and with his brothers. Acts 1:14 NIV

3.  The Prayer of Agreement:
Again, truly I tell you that if two of you on earth agree about anything they ask for, it will be done for the by my Father in Heaven. Matthew 18:19 NIV

4.  The Prayer of Request:
And pray in the Spirit on all occasions with all kinds of prayers and requests. With this in mind, be alert

and always keep on praying for all the Lord's people. Ephesians 6:18 NIV

5. The Prayer of Consecration and Dedication:

And he (Jesus) was withdrawn from them about a stone's cast, and kneeled down, and prayed, Saying, Father if thou be willing, remove this cup from me: nevertheless not my will, but thine, be done. Luke 22:41-42 KJV

6. The Prayer of Supplication:

Don't worry about anything; instead, pray about everything. Tell God what you need, and thank him for all he has done. Philippians 4:6 NLT

7. The Prayer of Thanksgiving:

Do not be anxious about anything, but in every situation, by prayer and petitions, with thanksgiving, present your request to God. Philippians 4:6 NIV

8. The Prayer of Worship:

While they were worshiping the Lord and fasting, the Holy Spirit said, "Set apart for me Barnabas and Saul for the work to which I have called them." So after they had fasted and prayed, they placed their hands on them and set them off. Acts 13:2-3 NIV

Note:  The "prayer of worship" is similar to the "prayer of thanksgiving." The "prayer of worship" focuses on who God is, and the "prayer of thanksgiving" focuses on what God has done.

9.  <u>The Prayer of Intercession</u>:

I exhort therefore, that, first of all, supplications, prayers, intercessions, and giving of thanks be made for all men: For kings, and for all that are in authority; that we may lead a quiet and peaceable life in all godliness and honesty. 1 Timothy 2:1-2 KJV The chapter of John 17 have prayers of Jesus praying on behalf of his disciples, verses 6 – 19, and all believers, verses 20 – 26.

10. <u>The Prayer of Binding and Loosing</u>:

Truly I tell you, whatever you bind on earth will be bound in heaven, and whatever you loose on earth will be loosed in heaven. Again, truly I tell you that if two of you on earth agree about anything they ask for, it will be done for them by my Father in heaven. For where two or three gather in my name, there am I with them. Matthew 18:18-20 NIV

11. <u>Prayer of Penitence</u>: This is a personal prayer asking for forgiveness of sin. Psalm 51 by King David is the best- known prayer of penitence in the Bible.

12. <u>The Prayer of Imprecation</u>: Imprecatory prayers are found in the Psalms 7, 55, 69 which was written by King David. They were used to invoke God's judgment on the wicked and his enemies.

Note: Jesus teaches us to pray blessing for our enemies, in the New Testament. You have heard that it was said, "Love your neighbour and hate your enemy. But I tell you, love your enemies and pray for those who persecute you, that you may be children of your Father in heaven. He causes his sun to rise on the evil and the good, and sends rain on the righteous and the unrighteous." Matthew 5:43-45 NIV

# Chapter 4

*The Sinner's Prayer*

The words "Sinner's Prayer" is an evangelical phrase. It refers to a prayer concerning repentance by an individual. In regards to the location of the "Sinner's Prayer" in the Bible, there isn't one mentioned; like the "Lord's Prayer" in Matthew 6. The "Sinner's Prayer" is stated indirectly based on Romans 10:9-10.

**That if thou shalt confess with
thy mouth the Lord Jesus,
and shalt believe in thine heart that God
hath raised him from the dead,
thou shalt be saved.
For with the heart man believeth
unto righteousness;
and with the mouth confession
is made unto salvation.**
Romans 10:9-10 KJV

I feel a need to elaborate briefly on "evangelical." The word "evangelical" has its origin from the Greek word for "gospel" or "good news" which gives a description of the life, miracles, death, and resurrection of Jesus Christ.

Evangelicals are Christians who believe in the "born again" experience in receiving salvation. **There was a man of the Pharisees, named Nicodemus, a ruler of the Jews: Jesus answered and said unto him, Verily, verily, I say unto thee, Except a man be born again, he cannot see the kingdom of God.** John 3: 1, 3 KJV

The Evangelical Christians also believe in the authority of the Bible as God's revelation to the human race and have a strong commitment to sharing the good news called "Evangelism." Evangelism gained considerable momentum in the 18th and 19th centuries. John Wesley, George Whitefield, Jonathan Edwards, Billy Graham, Harold Ockenga, John Stott and Martyn Lloyd-Jones were the leaders of the Evangelical Protest movement. The Reformed, Baptist, Wesleyan, and Pentecostal traditions have all had a strong influence within modern Evangelicalism.

The "Sinner Prayer" is also called the "Salvation Prayer." A "Sinner's Prayer" describes the words spoken in a prayer by an individual when he or she has recognized their sins and their need for a relationship with God through Jesus Christ.

What is sin? Merriam-Webster dictionary states that sin is an offense against religious or moral law, an action that is or is felt to be highly reprehensible, an often serious shortcoming, a transgression of the law of God. According to the Bible, it is any action that violates the law given by God in the Ten Commandments. Sin means to miss the mark, to fall short of the goal or standard set by God, committing unrighteous acts. The fact of the matter, we are all sinners.

> **As it is written: There is no one**
> **righteous, not even one:**
> Romans 3:10 NIV

> **As the Scriptures say, No one is**
> **righteous – not even one.**
> Romans 3:10 NLT

> **For all have sinned, and fall**
> **short of the glory of God:**
> Romans 3:23 NIV

> **Everyone has sinned; we all fall short**
> **of God's glorious standard.**
> Romans 3:23 NLT

The "Sinner's Prayer" takes various forms, shapes, and fashion. It can be a long prayer or a short prayer. There are no particular words that are considered essential, although it usually contains an admission of sin and a petition asking Jesus to forgive you and enter into your heart. Since it is regarded as a matter of one's personal will, it can be prayed in silently, aloud, read from a suggested guideline, or repeated after someone.

A similar "Sinner's Prayer" by Your Truly:
Father God, I know that I'm not living for you. I have sinned, and sin separates me from your presence. I am sorry for my sins, and I ask for your forgiveness. I know you have a much better plan and purpose for me. I have decided to accept Jesus as my savior. I want Jesus to abide, rule, and reign in my life from this day forward. I believe that your son, Jesus Christ died for my sins and was raised from the dead. He is alive and hears my prayer. Please send me your Holy Spirit, to help me in this Christian journey, give me the desire to obey You, and to do Your will. In Jesus' name, I pray, Amen.

A "Sinner Prayer" by the well-known Evangelist Billy Graham:
Dear Lord Jesus, I know that I am a sinner, and I ask for Your forgiveness. I believe You died for my sins and rose from the dead. I turn from my sins and invite You to come into my heart and life. I want to trust and follow You as my Lord and Savior. In Your Name. Amen.

Jesus Christ becomes your personal Lord and Savior when you repent. We need the following to grow closer with and in Our Lord and Savior:

1.  Get baptized as commanded by Christ, "And Jesus came and spake unto them, saying, All power is given unto me in heaven and in earth. Go ye, therefore, and teach all nations, baptizing them in the name of the Father, and of the Son, and of the Holy Ghost: Teaching them to observe all things whatsoever I have commanded you: and, lo, I am with you always, even unto the end of the world. Amen." Matthew 28:18-20

2.  Tell others about your faith in Christ, "But sanctify the Lord God in your hearts: and be ready always to give an answer to every man that asked you a reason of the hope that is in you with meekness and fear. 1 Peter 3:15. KJV

3.  Spend time in God's word each day, "Your word is a lamp to guide my feet and a light for my path. Psalm 119:105 NLT

4.  Ask God to increase your faith, the apostles said to the Lord, "Increase our faith!" Luke 17:5 NIV

5.  Fellowship with believers of Jesus, "Not forsaking the assembling of ourselves together, as the manner of some is; but exhorting one another: and so much the more, as ye see the day approaching. Hebrews 10:25 KJV

## Chapter 5

*The "Serenity Prayer"*

The American Theologian Reinhold Niebuhr is the author of the well-known "Serenity Prayer." He was also a minister, ethicist, political commentator, and a professor at the Union Theological Seminary for more than 30 years. Reinhold Niebuhr wrote several books with *Moral Man and Immoral Society* and *The Nature and Destiny of Man* being the most influential. The titles of the others are listed below:

1. *The Irony of American History*
2. *The Children of Light and the Children of Darkness*
3. *Leaves from the Notebook of a Tamed Cynic*
4. *An Interpretation of Christian Ethics*

Reinhold Niebuhr was born on June 21, 1892 in Wright City, Missouri. He is the son of German immigrants named Gustav and Lydia Niebuhr. His father was a German Evangelical Pastor. In 1915, Reinhold Niebuhr was ordained a pastor. He served at Bethel Evangelical Church in Detroit, Michigan with only 66 members. The congregation grew to nearly 700 members by the time he left in 1928. His church members consisted of blacks, whites, Jews, and Catholics. Pastor Niebuhr spoke out publicly against the Klan to his congregation. Reinhold Niebuhr was 78 years old when he died on June 1, 1971.

The "Serenity Prayer" is used in many and by many people, groups, and organizations. It has been adopted by Alcoholics Anonymous and adapted to address a broad range of substance abuse and dependency programs. Over 200 self-help organizations, often known as fellowship, now employ twelve-step principles for recovery. Just to name a few, some of the groups are Cocaine Anonymous, Crystal Meth Anonymous, Pills Anonymous, Marijuana Anonymous, Nicotine Anonymous, Gamblers Anonymous, Overeaters Anonymous, Sexual Compulsive Anonymous, Emotions Anonymous, Workaholics Anonymous,

The "Serenity Prayer" is also used by a cancer support group, in the novel/movie *The Fault in Our Stars* by John Green. It has been referenced twice in Kurt Vonnegut's novel, *Slaughterhouse-Five*. The prayer is repeated in Episode 7 of *The Wire*. It was recited by Marcia Cross' character, Bree, in Episode 20 of the 2nd season of *Desperate Housewives*.

The words of the "Serenity Prayer" can also be found in picture frames, hanging in many homes and offices. The "Serenity Prayer" words have been set to music by James MacMillan and Stratovarius. The song, "Feel So Different" written by Sinead O'Conner used the "Serenity Prayer'" words as the first line of the song.

The "Serenity Prayer" was communicated and circulated orally first; person to person, place to place, the city to city. The exact date it begins to circulate is not precise. In the "Serenity Prayer" we ask God to grant us the serenity to accept the things we can't change. We ask God to give us the courage to change the things we can change, and give us the wisdom to know the different.

Now, the earliest established date for a written form of the prayer various, also. It was printed in a newspaper articles in the early 1930's. Later, a pupil of Professor Niebuhr's named Winnifred Crane Wygal included the following version of the prayer in her book attributing it to Professor Niebuhr. The name of the book is "*We Plan Our Own Worship Services,*" and it was published in 1940.

O God, give us the serenity to accept
what cannot be changed,
The courage to change what can be changed,
And the wisdom to know the one from the other

Reinhold Niebuhr included the prayer in a sermon as early as 1943. Shortly after, it was included in a Federal

Council of Churches book for army chaplains. Niebuhr did not publish the "Serenity Prayer" until 1951 he printed it in one of his magazine columns.

Even though, the "Serenity Prayer" is used in 12-step recovery programs to help in the recovery process. It is important to understand that this prayer helps explain something we cannot change. We should be able to accept the things we cannot change and know what things we can change. This prayer is a challenge to all of us, not just those who are overcoming an addiction. The "Serenity Prayer" only 27 words long, but share words that we can, live, love, and learn by.

*just drop in my spirit, january 28, 2015 at 0846, glory, glory, hallelujah!*

Change starts from within and works its way out.

**I will give you a new heart and
put a new spirit in you:
I will remove from you your heart of
stone and give you a heart of flesh.
And I will put my Spirit in you and
move you to follow my decrees
And be careful to keep my laws.**
Ezekiel 36:26 -27 NIV

**And I will give you a new heart, and**
**I will put a new spirit in you.**
**I will take out your stony, stubborn heart**
**and give you a tender, responsive heart.**
**And I will put my Spirit in you so**
**that you will follow my decrees**
**and be careful to obey my regulations.**
Ezekiel 36:26-27    NLT


**P.S:**   Your truly, about to go to MacDonald; 0900 . . . .
Smile and pray


Jesus forever.

## Chapter 6

*The "National Day of Prayer"*

The "National Day of Prayer" is a day of observance held on the first Thursday of May. On that day, individuals of different faiths in the United States are asked, "to turn to God in prayer and meditation." It can be at a church, group gathering or done individually.

The United States has observed many unofficial national days of prayer throughout its history until 1952. The first unofficial "National Day of Prayer" was declared during the Continental Congress. The Continental Congress designated time for prayer in forming a new nation in 1775. It consisted of a convention of delegates from the Thirteen Colonies that became the governing body of the United States during the American Revolution in 1774.

In 1783, the conclusion of the Revolutionary War marked a temporary end to the "National Day of Prayer." Later, on February 19, 1795, President George Washington proclaimed a day of public thanksgiving and prayer. In 1813, President James Madison announced an officially day of prayer. He later said, "Such proclamations are not appropriate." In 1808, Thomas Jefferson also opposed declarations of the "National Day of Prayer."

On March 30, 1863, during the Civil War (1860-1865) Abraham Lincoln signed a Congressional resolution which called for a day of fasting and prayer. On April 17, 1952, a bill proclaiming an annual "National Day of Prayer" was unanimously passed by both houses of Congress. President Harry S. Truman signed it into law. However, the day and date was left to each President to select each year.

In 1988, Congress introduced a bill to set the day of the "National Day of Prayer. The first Thursday in May was the day set. The Senate bill, S 1378, was introduced by Strom Thurmond. It received sponsorship and support from both houses, and became Public Law 100-307. President Ronald Regan signed it into law on May 5, 1988, and commented, "On our National Day of Prayer, when, we join together as people of many faiths to petition God to show us His mercy and His love, to heal our weariness and uphold our hope, that we might live ever mindful of His justice and thankful for His blessing."

The "National Day of Prayer" is not a public holiday. The schools, post offices, stores and other businesses are open as usual. It invites people of faiths to pray for the nation. It communicates with every individual the need for personal repentance and prayer.

It asks the Christian's communities to intercede for America in six different areas which are listed below:

1. Our Nation: the President, his Cabinet members, Congress, the Court System and Judges
2. National and World Affairs: US Military, conflicts in the US and around the world
3. Our State and Local Governments: Governor, state legislators, mayors, and city councils
4. The Triangle: Universities, Schools, Law Enforcement, Firefighters, Rescue Workers, Businesses and Workplaces
5. Our Church: Leaders, missionaries, ministers and our church body
6. Our Families: Marriages, children, financial difficulties and health issues

**If my people,**
**which are called by my name,**
**shall humble themselves,**
**and pray,**
**and seek my face,**
**and turn from their wicked ways;**
**then will I hear from heaven,**
**and will forgive their sin, and will heal their land.**
2 Chronicles 7:14 KJV

At this moment, the next National Day of Prayer is 58:11:05:10 away which will be on Thursday May 7th, 2015.

**P.S:** I pray, I have this book finished by then, in Jesus' Precious Name. Amen.

## Chapter 7

*The Praying Hands*

The artwork of the "Praying Hands" is a pen-and-ink drawing that depicts a male with two hand palms together with it fingers stretched upward with partly up-folded sleeves revealed, circa 1508. The artwork is stored at Albertina Museum – Graphische Sammlung in Vienna, Austria.

The history behind the well-known "Praying Hands" starts in the fifteenth century, in a tiny village near Nuremberg, German. There lived a family with eighteen children. The father, Albrecht Durer the Elder was a goldsmith by profession. He worked almost eighteen hours a day at his trade merely to keep food on the table for his big family. He also worked other paying chores that he could find in the village.

Two sons of Albrecht Durer, the Elder, Albrecht and Albert, had dreams of studying at the Academy of Fine Arts in Nuremberg. They both wanted to pursue their love for art. However, they knew their father would never be financially able to send either of them to study at the Academy.

The two boys, Albrecht, and Albert finally made a pact. They would flip a coin to see who would so the Academy in Nuremberg, German, first. The loser of the coin toss would work the nearby mines. His earnings would be used to support his brother while he attended the academy for four years. Once he completed his studies, he would support his brother while he attended the academy. It would be done by the sales of his artwork or if necessary, by laboring in the mines.

They flipped a coin on a Sunday morning after church, and Albrecht Durer won and went off to Nuremberg. Albert worked in the dangerous mines, for the next four years. He financed his brother, at the Academy. The work of his brother, Albrecht was almost an immediate sensation. Albrecht's etchings, woodcuts, and oil works were far better those of most of his professors. He started earning considerable fees for his commissioned works, by the time he graduated.

The Durer family's held a dinner to celebrate Albrecht's triumphant homecoming. After the memorable meal, Albrecht rose from his honored position. He made a toast to his beloved brother, for the years of sacrifice that had enabled him to fulfill his ambition. Albrecht's closing words were, "And now, Albert, blessed brother of mine, now it is your turn. Now you can go to the

Academy in Nuremberg to pursue your dream, and I will take care of you."

Albert was sitting at the far end of the table, shaking his head from side to side, with tears rolling down his face repeating the word "no" over and over. Albert wiped the tears from his cheeks, as he glanced down the long table. Then Albert stated; he couldn't go to Nuremberg because every bone in my fingers has been shattered, at least once, and lately he has been suffering from arthritis. The arthritis is so badly in my right hand that he cannot even hold a glass to return his toast. Albert further stated, he wouldn't be able to make delicate lines on a parchment or canvas with a pen or a brush.

Albrecht Durer's has hundreds of masterful portraits, pen and silverpoint sketches, watercolors, charcoals, woodcuts, and copper engraving in almost every museum in the world. Most people are familiar with only one of Albrecht Durer's works, the "Praying Hands."

Albrecht wanted to pay homage to his brother Albert for all that he had sacrificed. Albrecht Durer with care and attention drew his brother's abused hands with palms together, and thin fingers stretched skyward. He called his drawing simply "Hands." The entire world opened their hearts to Albrecht masterpiece and renamed his tribute of love to his brother Albert the "Praying Hands."

## Chapter 8
*P * R * A * Y * E * R*

**Be careful for nothing;**
**but in every thing by prayer and supplication**
**with thanksgiving let your requests**
**be made known unto God.**
Philippians 4:6 KJV

An acronym for P*R*A*Y*E*R is what this chapter is concerning. I'm sure there are others, but this one is based on my learning at Jacksonville Theological Seminary, with a little, something added. I pray you enjoy it.

**P** - Prevailing
To prevail means to succeed, to achieve a victory. There are times when we must prevail in prayer as Jacob did. I have learned to achieve victory; sometimes it takes longer than a day, sometimes longer than a week or month. You have to pray, pray and pray until.

**"And he said, Thy name shall be called no more Jacob, but Israel: for as a prince hast thou power with God and with men, and hast prevailed."**
Genesis 32:28 KJV

**"Your name will no longer be Jacob," the man told him. "From now on you will be called Israel, because you have fought with God and with men and have won."** Genesis 32:28 NIV

**R** - **R**equesting

There are some Christians who fail to pray as they should until trouble strikes; I was one. We must pray, habitually.

**Ask, and it shall be given you; seek, and ye shall find; knock, and it shall be opened unto you:** Matthew 7:7 KJV

**"Keep on asking, and you will receive what you ask for. Keep on seeking, and you will find. Keep on knocking, and the door will be opened to you.** Matthew 7:7 NLT

**A** - **A**ccepting

Some Christians pray, but they fail to receive from God because they lack faith. We must ask with expectancy, accepting God's blessings by faith.

**Therefore I say unto you, What things soever ye desire, when ye pray, believe that ye receive them, and ye shall have them.** Mark 11:24 KJV

**Therefore I tell you, whatever you ask for in prayer, believe that you have received it, and it will be yours.** Mark 11:24 NIV

**Y** - **Y**ielding

Even though, Jesus was facing the challenge of dying on the cross; He yielded to His Father's will. Yield your will to God's will, He will strengthen you, answer prayers; but not necessary the way you would have like Him to.

**Saying, Father, if thou be willing, remove this cup from me: nevertheless not my will, but thine, be done.** Luke 22:42 KJV

**"Father, if you are willing, please take this cup of suffering away from me. Yet I want your will to be done, not mine."** Luke 22:42 NLT

**E** - **E**vangelizing

Our prayers can touch missionaries, loved ones, and the unsaved in the world. The prayer of faith is effective, both near and far. It will sustain and save people and places.

**Confess your faults one to another, and pray one for another, that ye may be healed. The effectual fervent prayer of a righteous man availeth much.** James 5:16 KJV

**Confess your sins to each other and pray for each other so that you may be healed. The earnest prayer of a righteous person has great power and produces wonderful results.** James 5:16 NLT

**R** - **R**ejoicing

Rejoicing comes with the anticipation of answered prayers. It is an act of faith that comes before the answer pray. We must praise the Lord before our prayers are answered, in the middle of our prayers being answered, and after our prayers are answered. God is worthy of the praise.

**Hitherto have ye asked noting in my name: ask, and ye shall receive, that your joy may be full.** John 16:24 KJV

**Until now you have not asked for anything in my name. Ask and you will receive, and your joy will be complete.** John 16:24 NIV

We have one question for this chapter . . . What does the suffix "ing" mean at the end of a word? Read slowly back over this chapter until you see the light. Smile and Pray . . . . . . . . . answer in the back of the book, no peeking.

# Chapter 9

*The Most Noticeable Prayers*

## Old Testament:

1. Abraham's Prayer for Sodom – Abraham's prays that God would spare Sodom from destruction, Genesis 18:23-33.
2. David's Prayer of Thanks – after God makes a covenant promise to David, he prays a prayer of thanks, 2 Samuel 7:18-29.
3. Solomon's Prayer of Dedication – After the work on the temple King Solomon dedicates the temple with prayer to God, 1 Kings 8:22-30.
4. Elijah's Prayer at Mount Carmel – He prays for God to reveal Himself to the people of Israel, 1 Kings 18:36-39.
5. King Hezekiah's Prayer – his prayer for deliverance from the invasion of Sennacherib King of Assyria, 2 Kings 19:15-19.
6. The Prayer of Ezra - he intercedes for the guilt and sin of the people, Ezra 9:5-15.
7. The Prayer of Jabez – Jabez prayed that God would to bless him, enlarge his territory, keep him from harm and be free from pain, 1 Chronicles 4:10.

8. Habakkuk's Prayer - the prophet Habakkuk prays a prayer of worship and rejoicing to the Lord, Habakkuk 3:1-19.

9. Hezekiah's Prayer – on his death-bed, Hezekiah cries out to God in prayer and God extends his life, Isaiah 38:2-8.

10. Daniel's Prayer – Daniel pleads for the Lord's mercy in petition and fasting for the captive Jews, Daniel 9:4-19.

## New Testament:

1. The Lord's Prayer – with this prayer Jesus taught his disciples how to pray, Matthew 6:9-13.

2. The Tax Collector's Prayer – the tax collector prays for mercy in a prayer of repentance, Luke18:13.

3. Christ's Intercessory Prayer - before going to the Father Jesus intercede for his disciples, John 17:6-19.

4. Stephen's Prayer at His Stoning – Stephen prayed while being stoned to death, intercedes for those throwing the stones, Acts 7:59-60.

5. Paul's Prayer for Spiritual Wisdom – Paul prays for spiritual wisdom and insight, Ephesians 1:15-23.

6. Paul's Prayer for Spiritual Growth - While in Ephesians, Paul bows to his knees in prayer for the spiritual growth of the Christian in Ephesus, Ephesians 3:14-21.

7. Paul's Prayer for Partners in Ministry – Paul prays for partners in ministry, Philippians 1:3-11.

8. Paul's Prayer for Knowing God's Will – The Apostle Paul prays for Christians to know God's will, Colossians 1:9-12.

9. A Prayer of Praise – Jude, the half-brother of Jesus, wrote a prayer of praise, Jude 1:24-25.

Let's see how many of the above prayers register in your soul?

## Old Testament

1. _____
2. _____
3. _____
4. _____
5. _____
6. _____
7. _____
8. _____
9. _____
10. _____

## New Testament

1. _____
2. _____
3. _____

4. _____

5. _____

6. _____

7. _____

8. _____

9. _____

P.S. Starting today, 3/24/2015 @ 1155, I'm going to print off each prayer in its entirety and read them every day, for least 40 days. Why not do the same? Even though, this assignment by Father was given to me, it wouldn't hurt if you did it with me. Excuse me for a few minutes.

For your convenience, I'm going to try to ease these 19 prayers in the back of the book in small print, with the hope of AuthorHouse approval. These are awesome, eye-opening, soul-throbbing, breathe-taking prayers. Praise God.

***Saturday, April 25, 2015 @ 0826; regrettably, this is one of the modifications, I had to make in this book. The 19 prayers in the back of this book have to be removed. Don't let this stop you from reading them in their entirety. You can read them from your iPad, iPhone or Bible. I truly feel you will have a better understanding about prayer and praying. Be Bless in Jesus' Name.

## Chapter 10

*Hour of Prayer*

Note: This chapter is from my book published on 10/24/2012, titled <u>Isaiah 26:3-4 "Perfect Peace III" Silver and Gold</u>, Chapter 3.

Now Peter and John went up together into the temple at **the hour of prayer**, being the ninth hour, Acts 3:1. These four words, "The Hour of Prayer," in the above Bible verse are unique and profound all by themselves. Oftentimes, we "read over" without truly understanding the depth of it. This chapter will expound on "The Hour of Prayer."

The three daily historic times of prayer in Biblical hours are specifically the third hour, the sixth hour, and the ninth hour of the day. These times were significant, respected and observed by the Old Testament Saints, the New Testament Church, and by the Lord Jesus Christ and the disciples.

> **Evening, and morning, and at noon**
> **will I pray, and cry aloud:**
> **and he shall hear my voice.**
> Psalm 55:17 KJV

41

| Evening: | Psalm 117 was read; only two verses. |
| Morning: | The Lord's Prayer, Matthew 6:9-13 was read. |
| Noon: | The Lord is my Shepherd, 23$^{rd}$ Psalm was read. |

(These three prayers are in the back
of book for your convenience)

The first hour of prayer is at 9am, called the 3$^{rd}$ hour. This is when the Temple gates are opened. The second hour of prayer is noon, called the 6$^{th}$ hour. It is also known as the "Hour of Confession." The third hour of prayer was at 3pm, called the 9$^{th}$ hour. The biblical days began at sundown, or about 6pm.

The Early Christians continued the Jewish practice of reciting prayers at certain hours of the day or night. In the book of Psalms, you will find expression like "in the morning I offer you my prayer," "At midnight I will rise," "Evening, morning, and at noon I will cry and lament," "Seven times a day I praise you."

Jesus' Apostles knew that prayer was a vital role in the believer's life. They even asked Jesus to teach them to pray.

**One day Jesus was praying in a certain place.**
**When He finished, one of his**
**disciples said to him,**
**"Lord teach us to pray, just as**
**John taught his disciple."**
Luke 11:1 NIV

Prayer is an essential element to God and man relationship to God. God said in Isaiah 56:7, "for my house will be called a house of prayer for all nations." In the Old Testament, the hours of prayer were known as the hours of "Sacrifice" or "Oblation," according to Daniel 9:21. Oblation is the act of offering something, such as worship or thanks, to a God.

**Yea, while I was speaking in prayer,**
**even the man Gabriel,**
**whom I had seen in the vision at the**
**beginning, being caused to fly swiftly,**
**touched me about the time of**
**the evening oblation.**
Daniel 9:21 KJV

The New Testament is filled with accounts of how God has honored these particular hours. It was the third hour on the day of Pentecost, when the 120 disciples were in the upper room praying for the promise of the Father, Acts 2:1-15.

**For these are not drunken, as ye suppose,**
**seeing it is but the third hour of the day.**
Acts 2:15 KJV

The New Testament Church customarily went to the temple at the hours of prayer. Peter and John went up together into the temple at the hour of prayer, being the ninth hour, Acts 3:1. On this occasion, a lame man was healed when the Apostle Peter took him by the hand and said, "Silver and gold have I none; but such as I have give I thee: In the name of Jesus Christ of Nazareth rise up and walk." Immediately, this man feet and ankle bones received strength; Acts 3:6-7. They were not at the temple by happenstance entering the temple but decidedly, deliberately and faithful doing so at the hour of prayer.

Now let's look at the biblical event of the Apostle Peter and Cornelius of Caesarea in Acts 10. Cornelius was a soldier in the roman army. Even though, he was a soldier for the roman's army, he was a righteous man who prayed to God always and was exceedingly generous in his almsgiving. He was in prayer about the ninth hour when an angel of the Lord appeared to him in a vision. The angel instructs Cornelius to send men to Joppa, and call for one Simon, whose surname is Peter.

The next day as Cornelius' servants came to Joppa, Peter had a spiritual experience. Peter was on the house rooftop praying about the sixth hour. Suddenly, he fell into a trance and saw a vision of a large linen cloth being let down from heaven full of all kinds of unclean beasts. God proceeded to tell Peter to receive these Gentiles because they had now been cleansed. This prepared Peter for ministry to the Gentiles people, whom he considered unacceptable for the kingdom of God. Peter obedience to God resulted in a great outpouring of the Holy Spirit upon the household of Cornelius and the Gentile nations.

The Seven Historical Hours of Prayer in reference to Psalm119 are listed below.

**Seven times a day
do I praise thee because of thy
righteous judgments.**
Psalm 119:164 KJV

| 6am- | First Hour | Psalm 5 |
|------|------------|---------|
| **9am-** | **Third Hour** | **The Lord's Prayer** |
| **Noon -** | **Sixth Hour** | **23rd Psalm** |
| **3pm-** | **Ninth Hour** | **Psalm 117** |
| 6pm- | Evensong | Psalm 150 |
| 9pm- | Compline | Psalm 4 |
| Midnight Prayers | | Psalm 119:62; Psalm 134 |

The observances of the three times a day prayer can serve as a reminder of our Lord's ultimate sacrifice of Himself on our behalf. The three prayers are related to the Crucifixion of Christ. Christ was crucified for us at the $3^{rd}$ hour. Then at the $6^{th}$ hour, darkness came over the land and lasted until the $9^{th}$ hour. At the $9^{th}$ hour is when our Lord gave up His spirit. Christ, our Passover, gave up His spirit at the time of the Evening Sacrifice.

**"And it was the third hour, and they crucified Him.
And the superscription of His
accusation was written over,
The King of the Jews."
"And when the sixth hour was come,
there was darkness over the whole
land until the ninth hour.
"And at the ninth hour Jesus
cried with a loud voice,
saying, Eloi, Eloi, Lama Sabachthani?
Which is, being interpreted, My God, My
God, why hast thou forsaken Me?"**
Mark 15:25, 33-34 KJV

In conclusion, prayer is significant at any hour of the day. God has given us prayer as a means of communion with and growing closer, to Him.

# Chapter 11

*The Praying Mantis*

One of the most loved insect by humans and the most feared to other insects are the Praying Mantis. They are extremely beneficial to gardens and humans because of its tendency to eat the things that bug us like, moths, bees, horseflies, and beetles. They eat mites, aphids, and other insects that are within their grasp. They will even attack and eat things much larger than them, like frogs and lizards. They will kill moths, bees, beetles and horseflies, which is what makes them loved by humans.

The Praying Mantis is related to the grasshoppers and crickets. They belong to a family of insects called orthopteran. There are about 1800 varieties of mantis, and most of them live in warm subtropical climate.

The United States has about three of types of the Praying Mantis which are the Carolina, European and Chinese. The Carolina mantis is a native to the United States while the European and Chinese Mantis arrived in the United States by shipments of goods in the late 1800's.

The female mantis is much larger than the male mantis, and sometimes the male mantis ends up as her lunch, especially when the mating ritual is over. The male mantises do not attempt to prevent themselves from being eating, but usually permit it.

The female carries her eggs with her before depositing them in a walnut sized cluster. The adult praying mantis grew well over 6 inches long. The praying mantis goes through several distinct changes as they grow from infancy to adulthood. The three changes which the mantis goes through as it changes from infancy to an adult are egg, nymph, and then adult.

Once the egg sack hatches, baby mantis are revealed. They are called nymph, and looks similar to their mothers, except they are a great deal smaller, and they don't have wings, yet. These little nymphs grow in a unique manner. Their skeletons are on the outside of their bodies. When the nymphs become too large, it shed the exoskeleton which is called molting. The baby mantis will lose this exoskeleton as many as ten times, depending on the species. When the last molting takes place, they emerge with wings. They will be thin, transparent and look a great deal like wrinkled fabric, but within several hours the wings will begin to stretch.

The insect was given the name "Praying Mantis" because of the way they hold their front legs in a praying position. The word "Mantis" is a Greek word for "prophet or seer." Praying Mantises are usually by themselves in a quiet location praying. It is important to pray regularly. Many of the priests, prophets, kings, men and women in the Bible prayed to God. Jesus himself prayed, and usually by himself.

In the Bible, people prayed to God for guidance, wisdom, strength, and peace.

## Chapter 12

*The Prayer Plant*

I can see it now, on our bathroom toilet tank cover, in a beautiful greenish and yellowish flower pot. Glory, Hallelujah! The Prayer Plant was/is my mom favorite plant. Oh my God, I just can't stop the tear from rounding down my cheeks. Gotta take a break . . . 03/13/2015 @ 0645.

The "Prayer Plant" belongs to the Marantaceae Family. The Marantaceae Family is flowering plants known for its large underground starchy rhizomes. They are sometimes called the Pray-Plant Family. It is suggested that there are 1,536 species in this family of plants. They thrive in very hot and humid area of the world. They are a native to Brazil.

The scientific name of the "Prayer Plant" is Maranta Leuconeura. The "Prayer Plant" is named after Bartolomeo Maranta. He was an Italian Physician and Botanist and Literacy Theorist of the 16th century.

The "Prayer Plants" are evergreen perennials and are low-growing ground covers outdoors. The plants usually have underground rhizomes or tubes. The plant light –green leaves are oval and grow about 6 inches long and 3 inches wide. The leaves are marked with red veins on some variety and dark spots on others. The pinkish flower is insignificant. The Maranta Leuconeura produces foliage with dark brown green blotches between the veins, resembling rabbit footprints.

It is an interesting natural phenomenon where a plant moves by itself. The "Prayer Plant" is best known for its habit of folding up it 6 by 3 inch leaves at night. The "Prayer Plant" folds and bends upward at night, giving them the appearance of praying hands. It leaves opens in the morning sometimes making a rustling sound.

The "Prayer Plants" are also grown indoors. They are seemed planted in hanging baskets and small containers on the porch. A prayer plant rarely blooms indoors, but sometimes grows tiny, white or pinkish tubular flowers on long stems. The flowers are insignificant; it is the magnificent leaves that are the attraction.

The "Prayer Plant" takes a rest during winter and growth will slow down. Keep the soil dry, by spraying the plant daily with warm water. The plant can be placed on top of a shallow bowl of pebbles and water, but do not allow the plant to sit in the water.

There are several varieties of Maranta. The Maranta Erythrophylla and Maranta Kerchoveans are the most popular. Many Marantas are rare and hard to find according to the Union County College. Listed below the names of some Marantas are named and descripted:

1.  Tricolor (Maranta Leuconerura "Erthrophylla") – The leaves are dark green in three shades, with scarlet vein and patches of light cream or yellow variegation.
2.  Silver Feather (Maranta Leuconeura "Leuconerura") – This variety of Maranta is rare but showy. This "Prayer Plant" leaves has a light gray center, with a dark green border, and from the center are silvery veins.
3.  Bicolor (Maranta Leuconerus "Bicolor) – Maranta bicolor is another rare variety. This plant has dark green upper leaves with light green splotches with the undersides being a rich purple color. .
4.  Rabbit Tracks (Maranta Leuconerura "Kerchoviana") – The rabbit's tracks variety of Maranta has a unique pattern on the leaves. The leaves are light and dark green or brown, sometimes with red or gray veins. The underside is gray-green marked with reddish purple.

The "Prayer Plant" sometimes called "Praying Hands" needs to be in a well-drained soil and requires high humidity to thrive. Clean dust from "Prayer Plant" leaves with a soft, moistened cloth to reduce mites. Slugs, roundworms and root decay are other pests that affect the "Prayer Plant." When grown indoors, these issues are rare, except for root decay, but it can be avoided by using a well drain soil.

The "Prayer Plant" will live for many years with excellent care.

I'm going buy one today in honor of the memories of my MOM, and place it on the living room table. The one I kept after her passing into Glory, died many, many years ago. Thank you, God Father for bringing this lovely remembers back to me. You are so Awesome. @1031 03/28/2015

**P.S: Holliday Flowers & Events, Inc. had to order a "Prayer Plant" for me. Phyllis said, "It will be ready for me to pick up Monday evening."**

## Author's Closing Remarks

**On My Heart . . .**

This book offers a unique and innovative way to keep your mind on the Lord, more. Hopefully, a particular object, thing or item mention in this book will at least, prompt you to think about prayer.

Praying consistently will change your life. I believe your prayers will be truly effective if you commit to these four principles which are Praise, Repent, Ask and Yield.

As this book ministry come to a close . . . Will You Pray for the Ministry . . . "Now, and Out Loud" Hallelujah!

May the "LORD of Peace," Himself give you Peace, "His Perfect Peace" and be with you. Amen.

Dr. Vanessa

# References

Chapter 1

1. Answers: http://www.answers.com/Q/How_many_times_is_pray_mentioned_in_the_King_James_Bible

Chapter 2

1. Wikipedia, the Free Encyclopaedia: http://www.en.wikipedia.org/wiki/Lord%27s_Prayer

Chapter 3

What are the types of prayer? http://www.gotquestions.org/types-of-prayer.html

Chapter 4

1. Evangelicalism: http://www.en.wikipedia.org/wiki/Evangelicallism
2. Finding Hope in Jesus Christ – My Hope with Billy Graham http://www.findingmyhope.org

Chapter 5

The Serenity Prayer: http://www.enwikipedia.org/wikie/Serenity_Prayer

Chapter 6

1. The National Day of Prayer: http://en.wikipedia.org/wiki/National_Day_of_Prayer

2. The National Day of Prayer: http://www.crossroads. org/story.aspx?storyid=460

3. History of the NDP: http://www.religioustolerance. org/day_pray2.htm

Chapter 7

1. The Praying Hands: http://www.moytura.com/ reflections/prayinghands.htm

Chapter 8

1. P*R*A*Y*E*R: From my studies at Jacksonville Theological Seminary.

Chapter 9

The Most Noticeable Prayers

1. The Hours of Prayer/ Biblical Times of Memorial: http://www.arenessministry.org/biblicialhours ofprayer.htm

2. The Seven Historical Hours of Prayer: http://prayerfoundation.org/dailyoffice/the_seven_ hours_of_prayer.htm

Chapter 10

1. Hour of Prayer: This chapter is taken from Isaiah 26:3-4 "Perfect Peace III" Silver and Gold, Chapter 3; from my book published on 10/24/2012.

Chapter 11

1.  Praying Mantis: http://www.itsnature.org/ground/crpt-crawlies-land/praying-mantis/

Chapter 12

1.  Prayer Plant:
http://www.gardenguides.com/11756-prayer-plant-varieties.html

# Answers & Information:

Chapter 1

1. Earnestly: showing or expressing sincerity or seriousness.
2. Ten Commandments
   1. You shall have no other gods before Me,
   2. You shall not make idols.
   3. You shall not take the name of the LORD your God in vain.
   4. Remember the Sabbath day, to keep it holy.
   5. Honor your father and your mother.
   6. You shall not murder.
   7. You shall not commit adultery.
   8. You shall not steal.
   9. You shall not bear false witness against your neighbour.
   10. You shall not covet.

Chapter 8

"ing" added to the end of a word means that particular WORD is BEING DONE; it turns into an Act.

Chapter 10

**The Three Daily Historic Prayers:**

**Psalm 117** [1] Praise the LORD, all you nations; extol him, all you peoples. [2] For great is his love toward us, and the faithfulness of the LORD endures forever. Praise the LORD.

**Psalm 23 A psalm of David.** [1] The LORD is my shepherd, I lack nothing. [2] He makes me lie down in green pastures, he leads me beside quiet waters, [3] he refreshes my soul. He guides me along the right paths for his name's sake. [4] Even though I walk through the darkest valley, I will fear no evil, for you are with me; your rod and your staff, they comfort me. [5] You prepare a table before me in the presence of my enemies. You anoint my head with oil; my cup overflows. [6] Surely your goodness and love will follow me all the days of my life, and I will dwell in the house of the LORD forever.

**Matthew 6:9-13** [9] After this manner therefore pray ye: Our Father which art in heaven, Hallowed be thy name. [10] Thy kingdom come, Thy will be done in earth, as it is in heaven. [11] Give us this day our daily bread. [12] And forgive us our debts, as we forgive our debtors. [13] And lead us not into temptation, but deliver us from evil: For thine is the kingdom, and the power, and the glory, for ever. Amen.

## Other books by the author:

From the Pew to the Pulpit

Isaiah 26:3-4 "Perfect Peace"

Isaiah 26:3-4 "Perfect Peace" The Last Single Digit

Isaiah 26:3-4 "Perfect Peace III" Silver and Gold

Isaiah 26:3-4 "Perfect Peace IV" The Kingdom Number

Isaiah 26:3-4 "Perfect Peace V" 2541

Isaiah 26:3-4 "Perfect Peace VI" Zacchaeus

Isaiah 26:3-4 "Perfect Peace VII" Eleven